INDEPENDENT SCHOOL DISTRICT #564
THIEF RIVER FALLS, MINNESOTA

Acquired Under
TITLE II, P.L. 89-10

About the Book

When the American people—adults and children alike—learned that wild horses were becoming extinct and were without legal protection, they rallied to the cause. As a result of their many thousands of letters to Representatives and Senators, a bill to protect wild horses was passed in 1971. In their letters, many boys and girls expressed the regret that they would probably never see a wild horse, but they added that they wanted them protected anyway.

This book provides an opportunity to see a typical band of wild horses and to learn something about their habits. The social life of the wild horse is organized around a harem of mares dominated by a single stallion. The stallion and his mares have definite roles to perform which ensure the survival of the band. These photographs depict the roles accurately. Some of the horse behavior may impress the reader as being beyond what he has been led to expect of animal intelligence.

The photographs were taken of an actual band of wild horses that roam freely on 4,000 acres of native prairie in eastern Wyoming. These horses are protected by the Robert Brislawn family of Oshoto, Wyoming, and are judged by the Spanish Mustang Registry to be pure descendants of the Spanish Barb horses lost by the conquistadors in the sixteenth century. For fifty years octogenarian brothers, Robert and Ferdinand Brislawn, have combed wilderness areas in search of animals that resembled the original Spanish mustang. With the help of Robert's son, Emmett, selected animals were captured, registered in the Spanish Mustang Registry, and then released to run free on the Cayuse Ranch True Blood Reserve. There the horses resumed their wild life, foraging for themselves in summer and winter. The stallions on the reserve must battle for their own mares, and the strongest stallions win the largest harems.

The black stallion in the book was captured out of the Bookcliff Mountains in Utah in 1969, when he was approximately five years old. During his first year on the reserve he remained a lone stallion. The following year he challenged other stallions for mares and successfully gathered eleven females. These are his first colts.

the Wild Colt

The Life of a Young Mustang

Written and Photographed by **HOPE RYDEN**

Coward, McCann & Geoghegan, Inc.
New York

ACKNOWLEDGMENTS

I wish to thank Gioja and Emmett Brislawn for their hospitality at the Cayuse Ranch during the many days that I observed and photographed the wild colt.

I also wish to express my gratitude to Robert and Ferdinand Brislawn for having the vision to gather and protect some Spanish mustangs so that future generations might know this animal.

I am also grateful to Stacy Pennebaker for her long hours of labor in the darkroom printing these pictures.

Second Impression

SBN: TR 698-20178-7
Copyright © 1972 by Hope Ryden
All rights reserved. This book, or parts thereof, may not be reproduced in any form without permission in writing from the publishers. Published simultaneously in Canada by Longmans Canada Limited, Toronto.
Library of Congress Catalog Card Number: 73-187138
PRINTED IN THE UNITED STATES OF AMERICA
04208

To the Brislawn family

The wild colt was the color of pale sand. His mane and tail were as black as a crow's wing. And around each leg he had stripes like bracelets. He also had a black band down his back and two across his shoulders. With so many stripes he looked a little like his relative the wild zebra.

The wild colt was a member of a band of wild horses that ran free and looked after themselves. Because no one owned them, they did not have to pull wagons or carry burdens on their backs. They could live as they pleased. They could be themselves.

But because no one owned them, they had to be responsible for themselves. No one fed them. And so they had to search for their own food and water and defend themselves from enemies.

The wild colt's mother was very satisfied with her beautiful colt. She knew the best ways to take care of him. She needed no help from man.

Because she was wild, she had never been brushed, and the front part of her mane was stuck together with cockleburs.

The wild colt's father was a black stallion. He was the only adult male, or stallion, in the wild horse band, and he was in charge. All the other grown horses were females, or mares. A group of mares is called a harem. Of course, there were several young male colts in the horse band, but there was only one grown stallion.

The wild colt had several half brothers and sisters. The black stallion was father to all the colts. But each colt had his own mother. And each colt had his own ways.

Every mare took care of her own colt. This was the wild colt's youngest brother.

Two colts in the band were especially good friends and played together all the time. It is not unusual for one horse to choose another as his own special companion. Such friendships show clearly the sociable nature of horses.

Still another of the wild colt's brothers was especially adventuresome. He liked to wander off by himself. His mother was constantly having to herd him back into the band.

The wild colt had only one sister, a filly. A filly is a female colt. Like her brother, this filly had zebra stripes around her legs too. Wild horses that have such stripes are thought to have lived and bred in the wilderness for many generations.

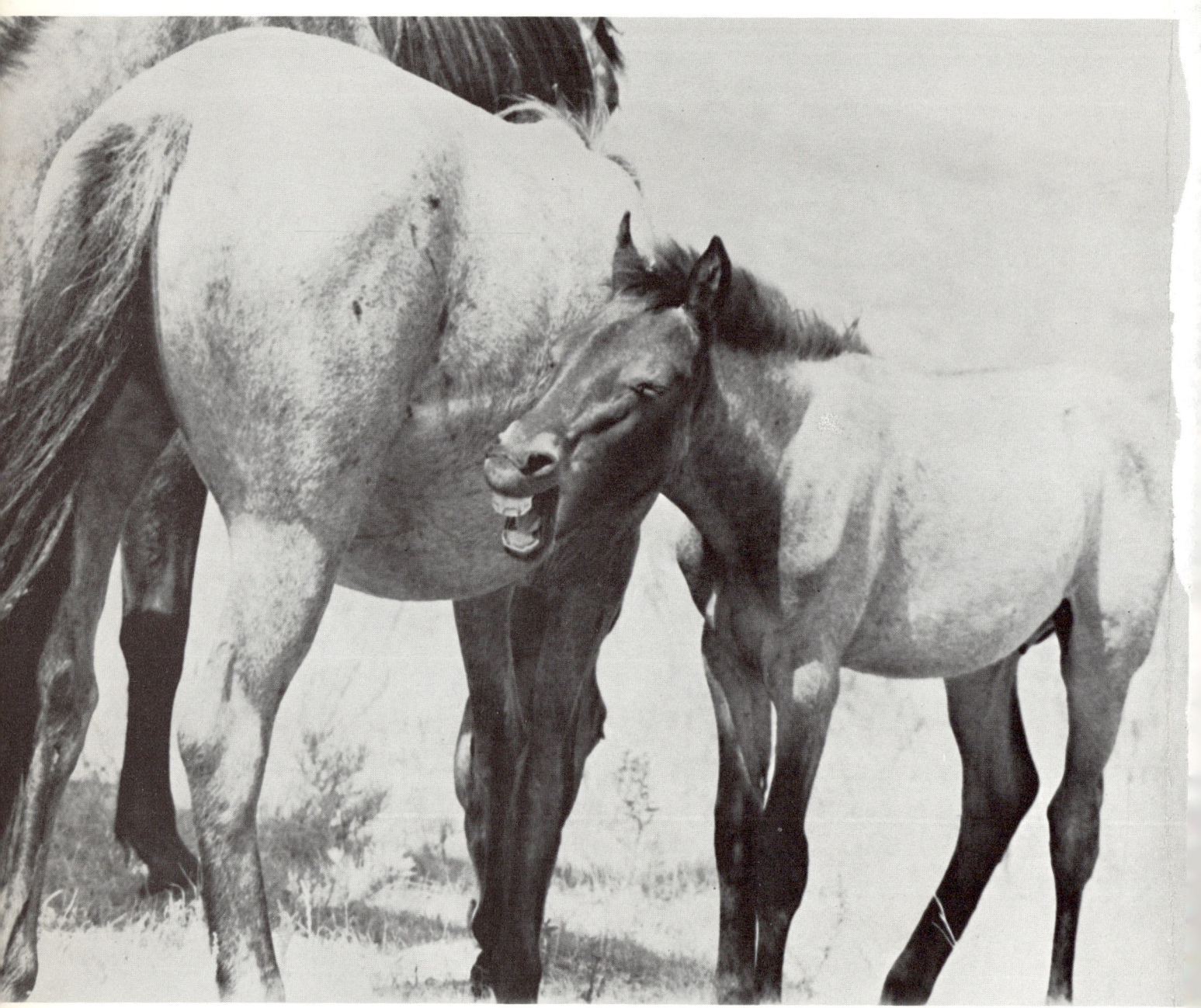

The noisiest colt in the wild horse band was the blue roan. He whinnied nearly all the time and annoyed some of the mares.

A roan horse has a beautiful peppery coat made up of black and white hairs which shine blue in the sunlight.

These were the brothers and sisters of the wild colt.

But the wild colt had not always lived in the harem with his mother and father, six brothers and sisters, and ten aunts. Just before he was born, his mother left the wild horse band and searched for a brushy place where she could hide a newborn foal. A foal is a very young colt. There the wild foal was born.

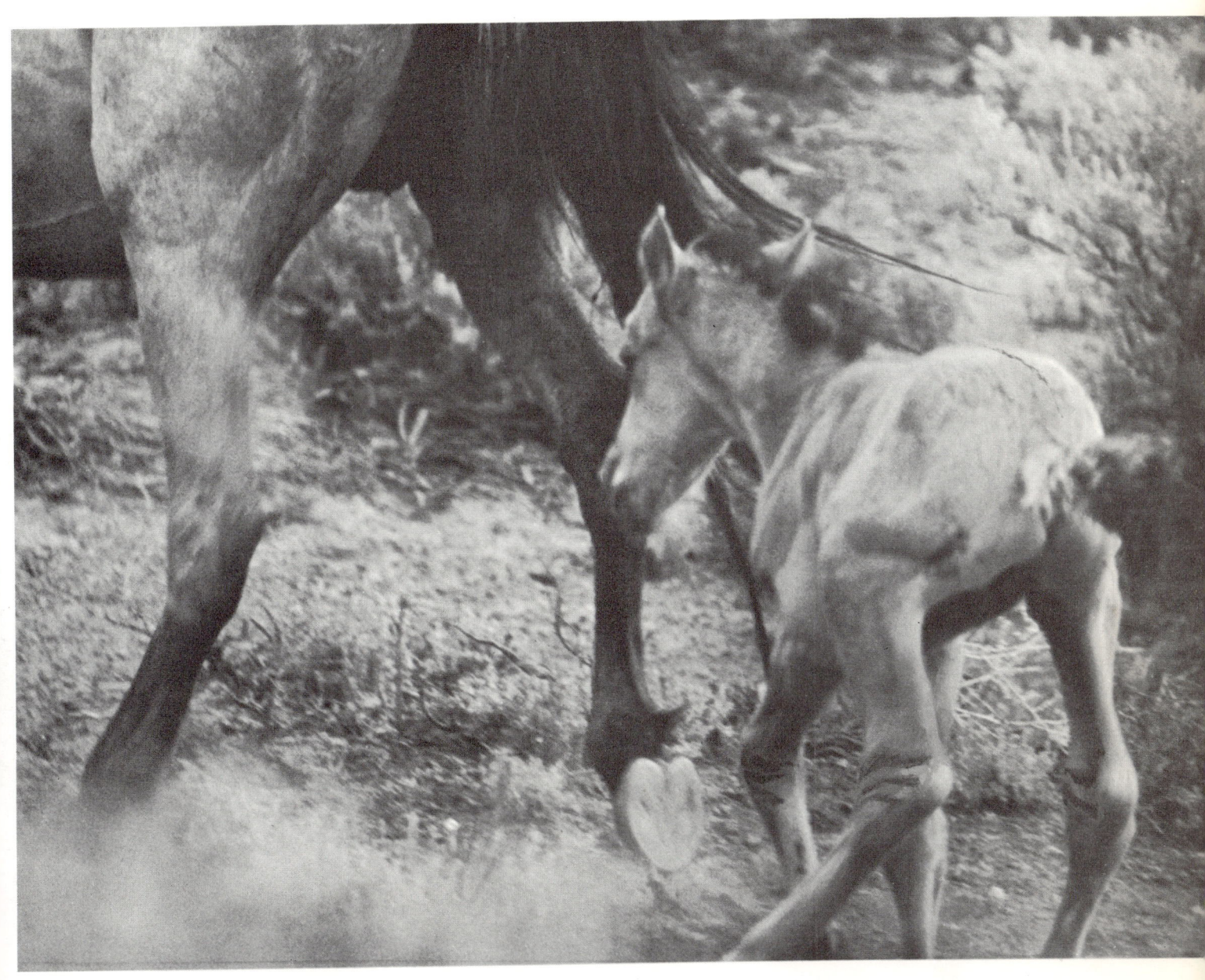

When the baby was strong enough to stand on his feet and travel, he followed his mother back to the harem.

Life in the wild horse band was good. The wild colt spent a great deal of time resting...

. . . and he spent a great deal of time eating.

Sometimes he and his mother groomed each other.

And on days when the flies were especially troublesome, the mare brushed them off his face with her long tail.

Being a wild colt was fun. One of his brothers or sisters was always getting up a game of chase. And the wild colt was not one to sit by himself on the sidelines and watch.

When he saw a game starting, he got into it.

Their spirited, reckless, and rollicksome play was not only fun, but good exercise for wild colts who were full of milk and prairie grass.

ST. HILAIRE SCHOOL LIBRARY
St. Hilaire, Minnesota

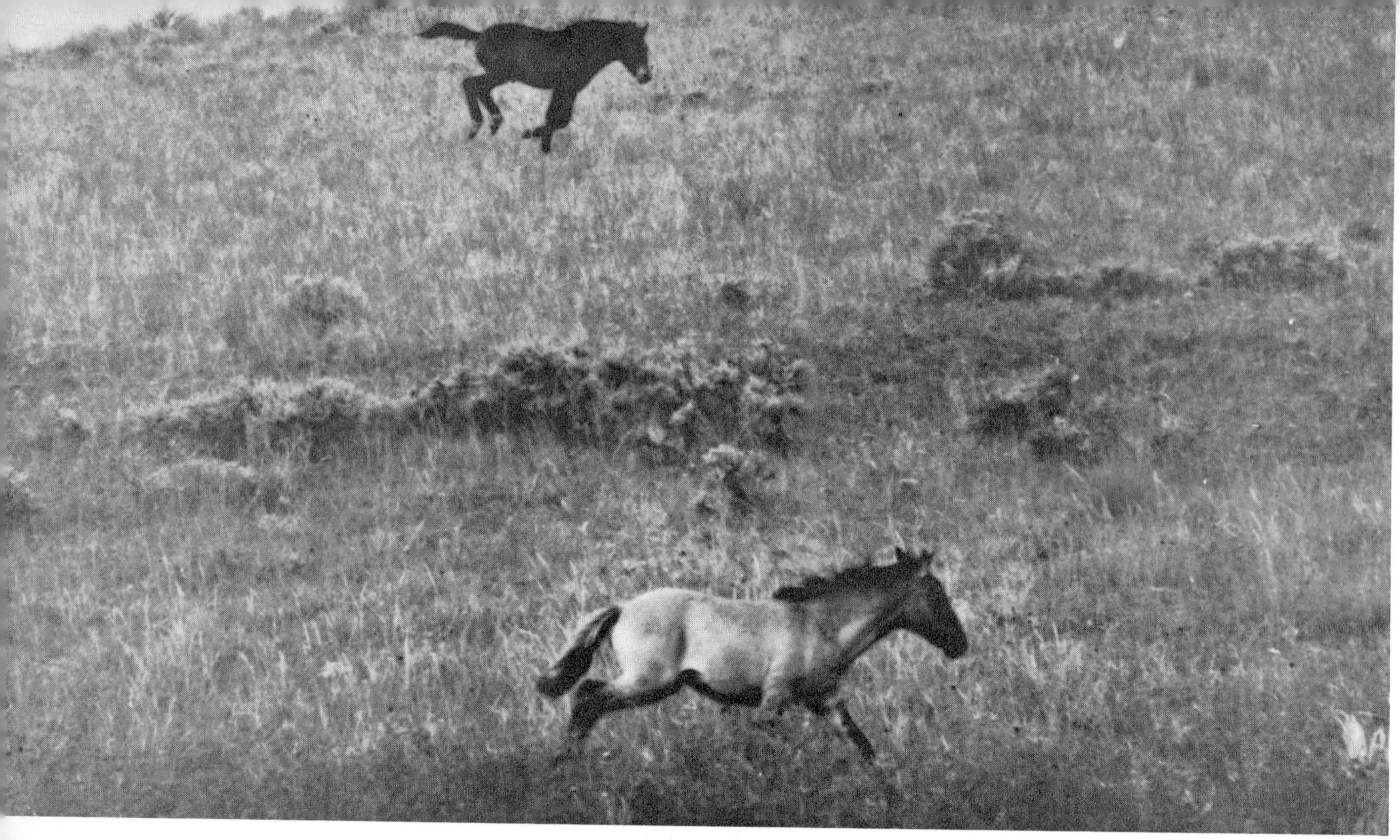

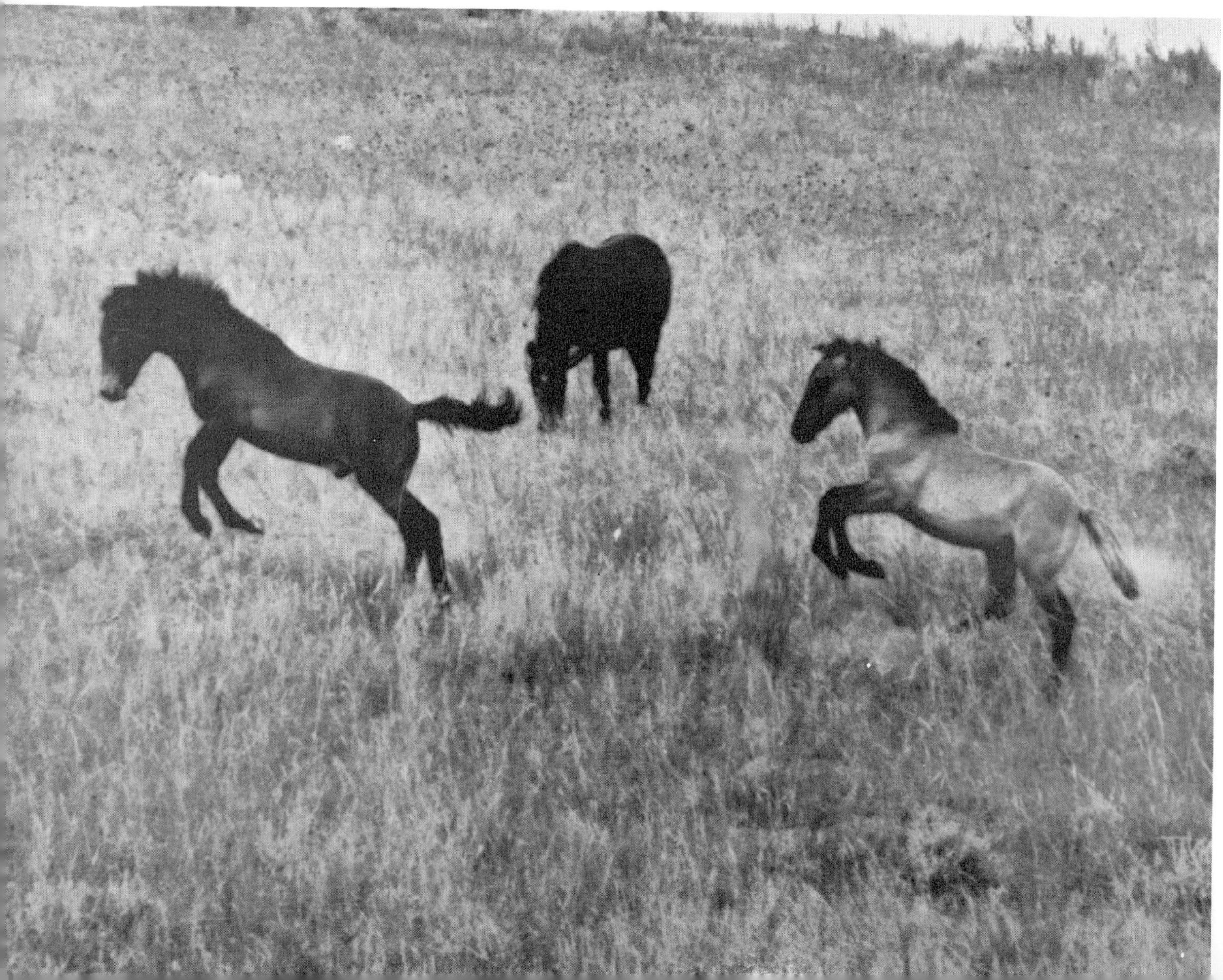

Sometimes a game was so exciting that the wild colt didn't want it to end. Then his playmate's mother had to shoo him away...

... or his own mother had to call him over to her.

Sometimes the wild colt played with his father.

Not every wild stallion will pay attention to his young offspring. But the black stallion played with his colts nearly every day.

He even allowed his young son to pull cockleburs out of his mane.

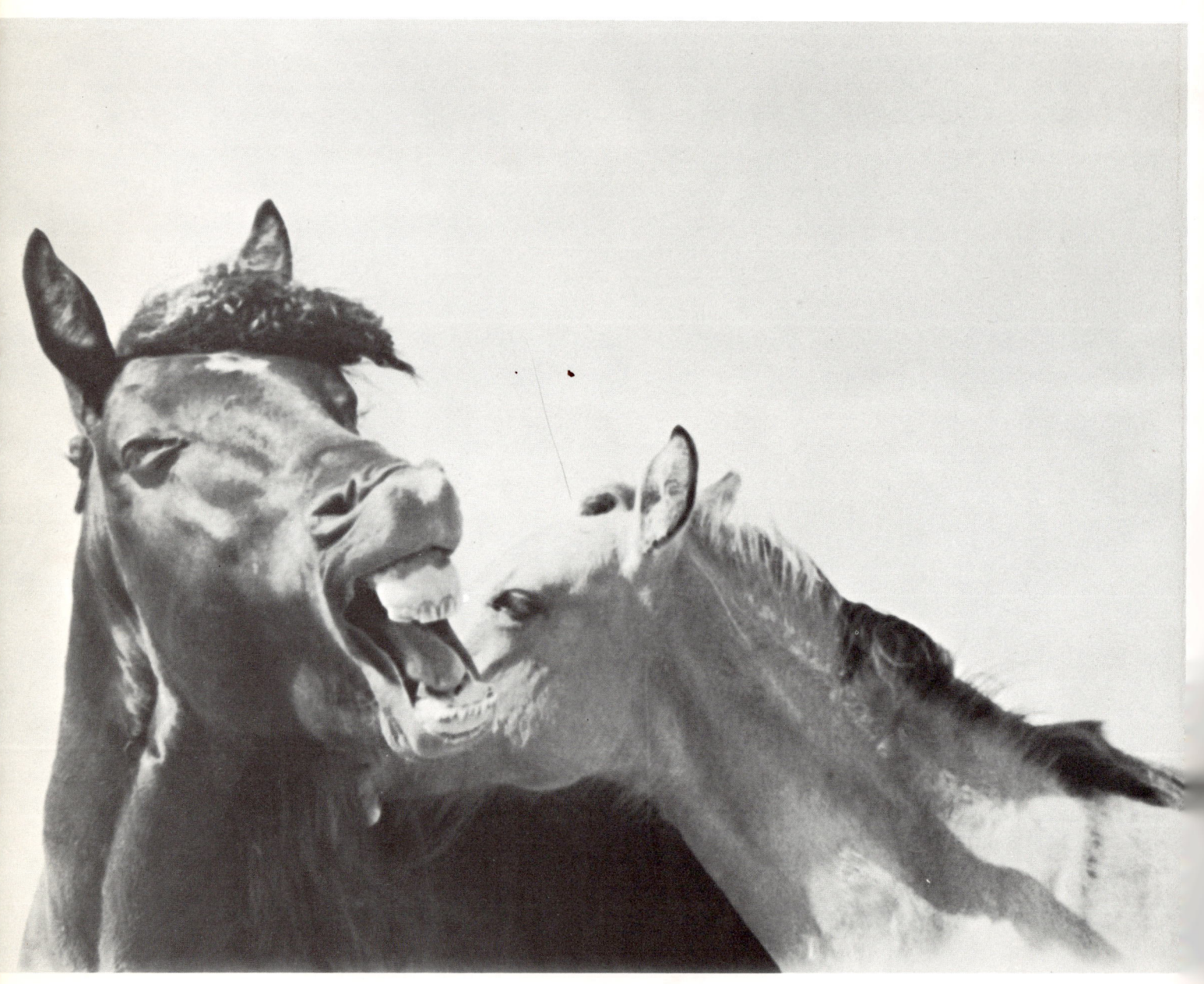

And judging by his reaction, he seemed to enjoy it. When wild horses open and close their mouths like this, Westerners say they are "mixing medicine." It is a way the horse communicates his pleasure.

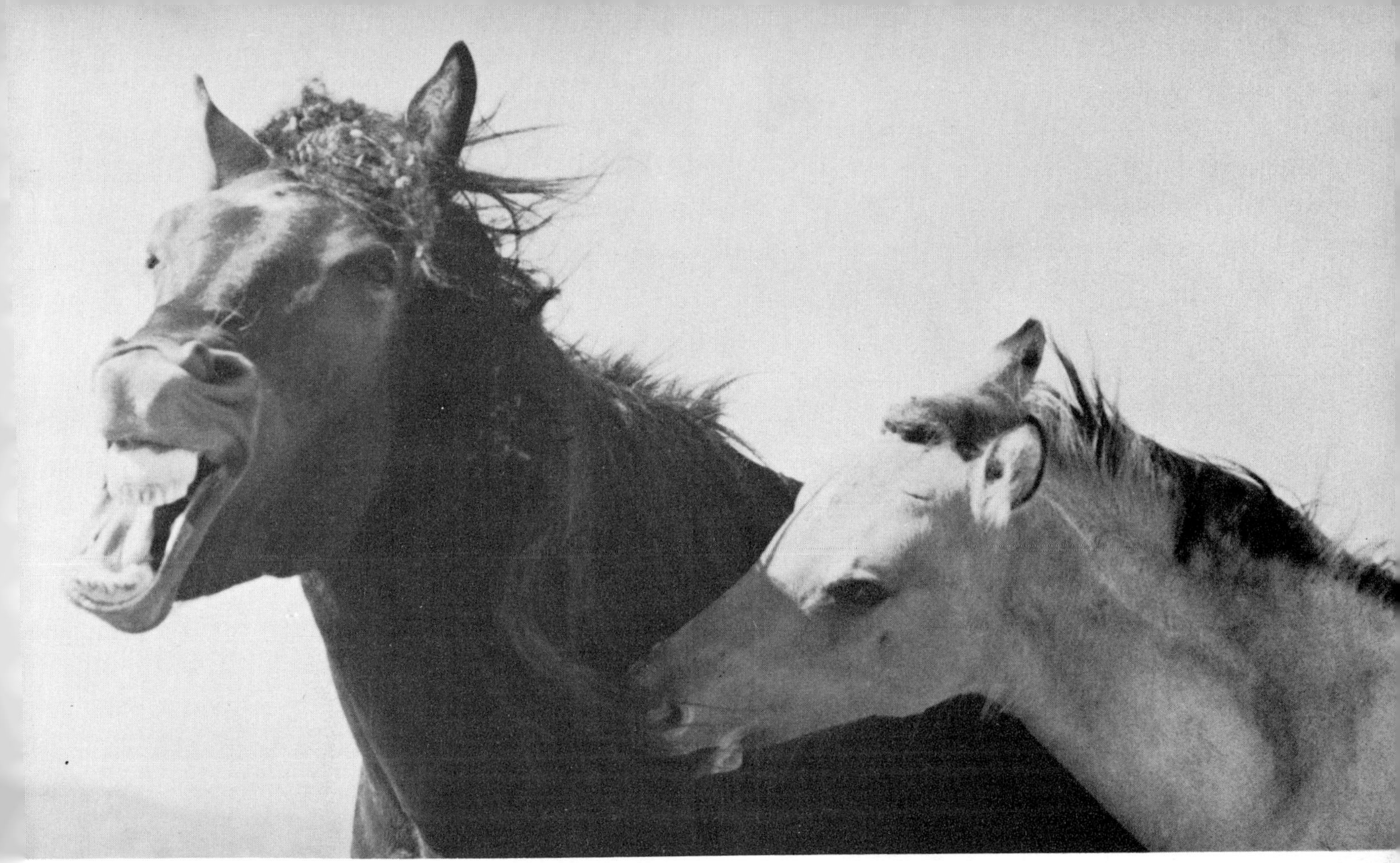

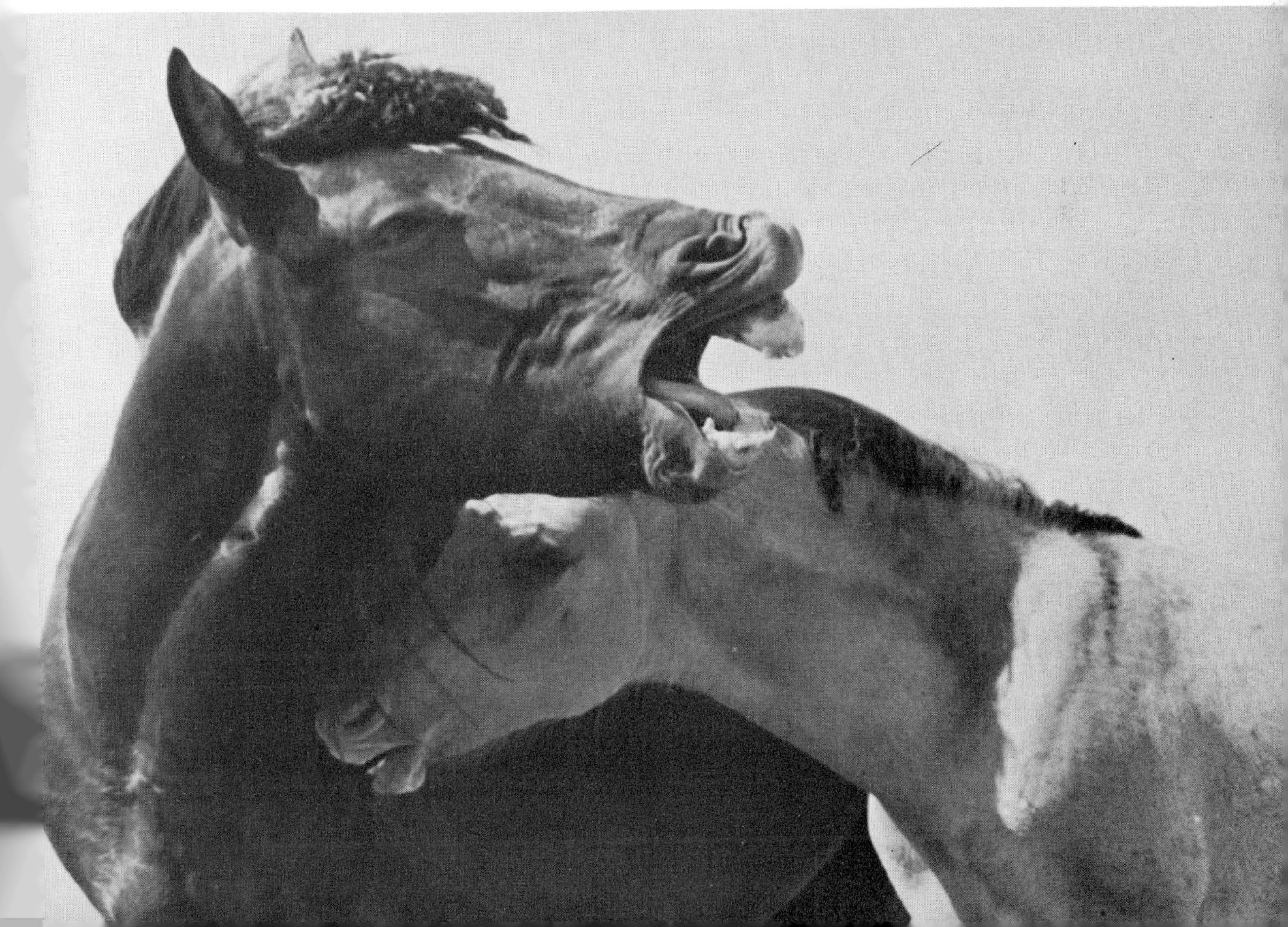

The wild horse band grazed in a special area that was its territory. The stallion allowed no other wild horses to use this land, but he did not chase away deer or antelope.

While his band of mares and colts grazed, the black stallion stood guard and watched for enemies. This was his most important role.

The stallion's watchfulness made life safer for the mares and colts. When his harem moved from place to place, he always walked last in line. If an enemy tried to stalk the wild horses, he would wheel about and fight the attacker while his mares and colts ran ahead to safety.

The wild horses made a trip to water nearly every day.

But when there was no rain, the water hole dried up. Then the stallion and the other wild horses had to dig in the creek bed until water seeped to the surface.

After the wild horses had churned up a spring and finished watering themselves, other thirsty animals could come to drink. Opening up water holes is one of the ways in which wild horses are useful to other animals.

But in the spring and early summer the water hole brimmed with water, and the wild horses spent long hours grazing along its cool bank. The plants that grew there were especially green and juicy to eat.

Sometimes the wild colt practiced digging along the wet bank. Here it was easy to make holes that quickly filled up with water.

The world was new to the little colt, and he was interested in everything he saw. He picked up sticks ... smelled flowers ...

. . . and even investigated the litter that man had carelessly left in the wilderness.

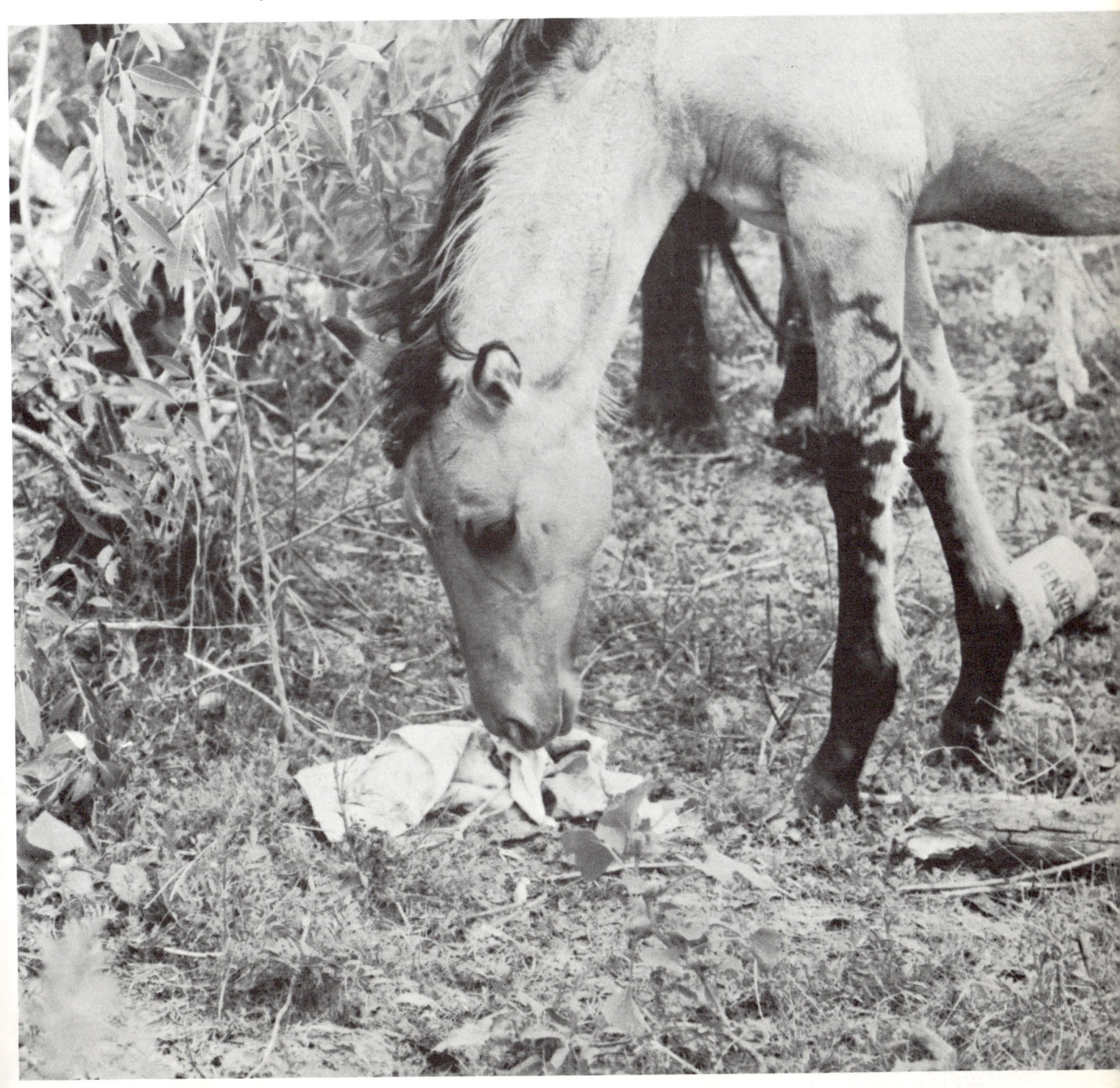

One day the wild colt heard a strange squealing noise.
He looked around to see what could be making the racket.

A black-tailed prairie dog was sitting on his haunches, sounding a warning. Nearby several prairie dogs scurried into holes in the ground.

The wild colt was curious about the strange little animal. He had never seen a prairie dog before.

The prairie dog was curious about the wild colt, too. But he was not very brave. When the wild colt came toward him, the prairie dog popped into a hole in the ground.

The wild colt did not see the prairie dog vanish into the burrow, and he galloped right across the hole and kept on going. After a while he came to a fence. He was now outside the territory of the wild horse band. And he was dangerously close to the territory of a rancher.

The stallion noticed that the colt had strayed and he went to gather him. Though the rancher who happened to live alongside this band of wild horses would not have harmed the little colt, many men have been cruel to wild horses. So wild horses avoid men.

Now the little colt was being taught a lesson. Something in the stallion's nature made him keep his band together at all times.

So he pulled the little colt by the tail . . .

. . . and nosed him back to the harem.

Not much escaped the notice of the wild stallion. At the first sign of danger, he sent his mares and colts running. Then he would turn back to face the enemy.

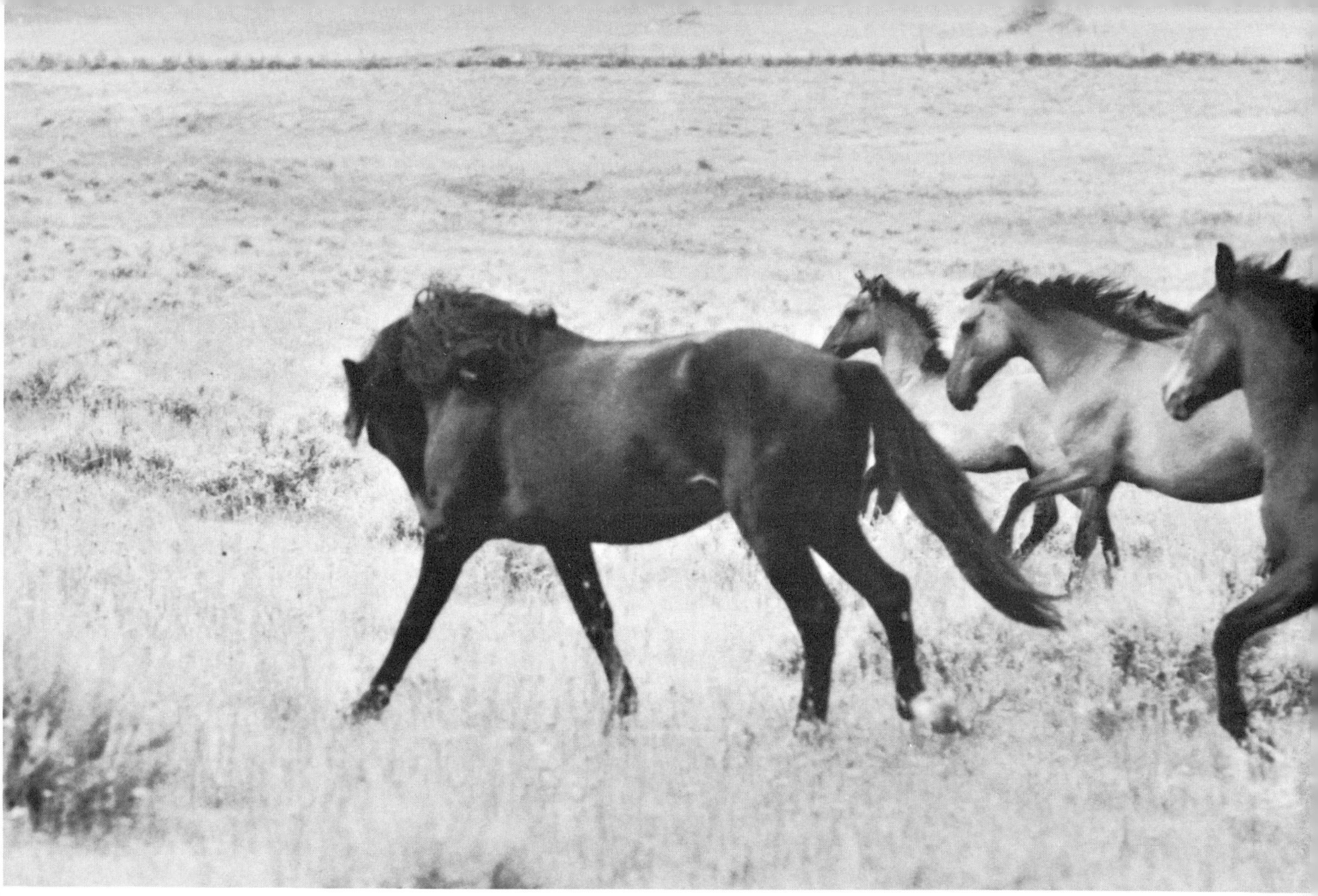

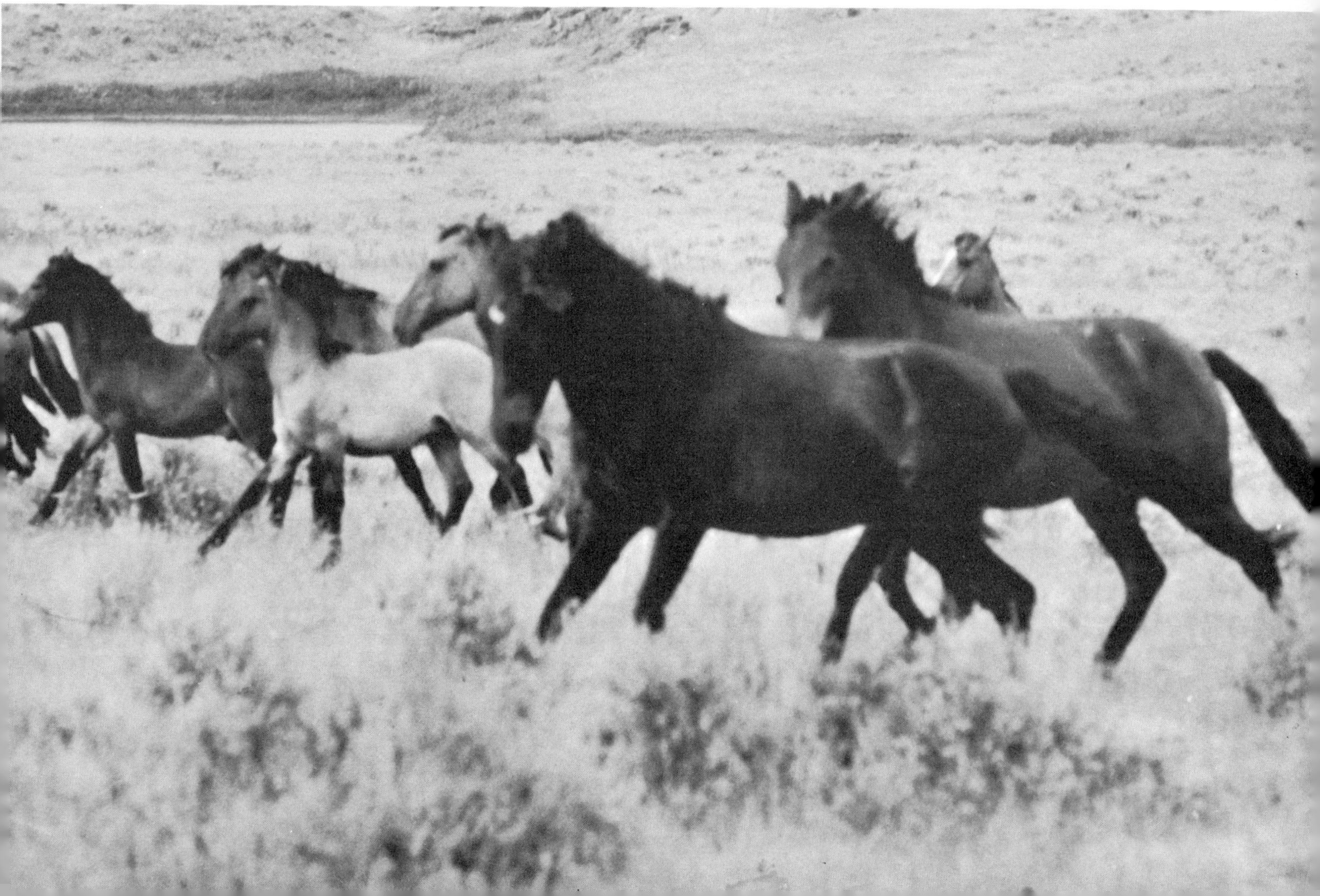

Usually the enemy was another stallion who was trying to capture a mare or two from the black stallion's harem. The two male horses would fight it out.

When the black stallion had succeeded in chasing away his rival, he would catch up with his fleeing band.

The little colt's mother was also alert for signs of danger.

When something roused her suspicion, she nudged her little colt and sent him running.

From dawn to dusk the wild mare guarded and fed her little colt.

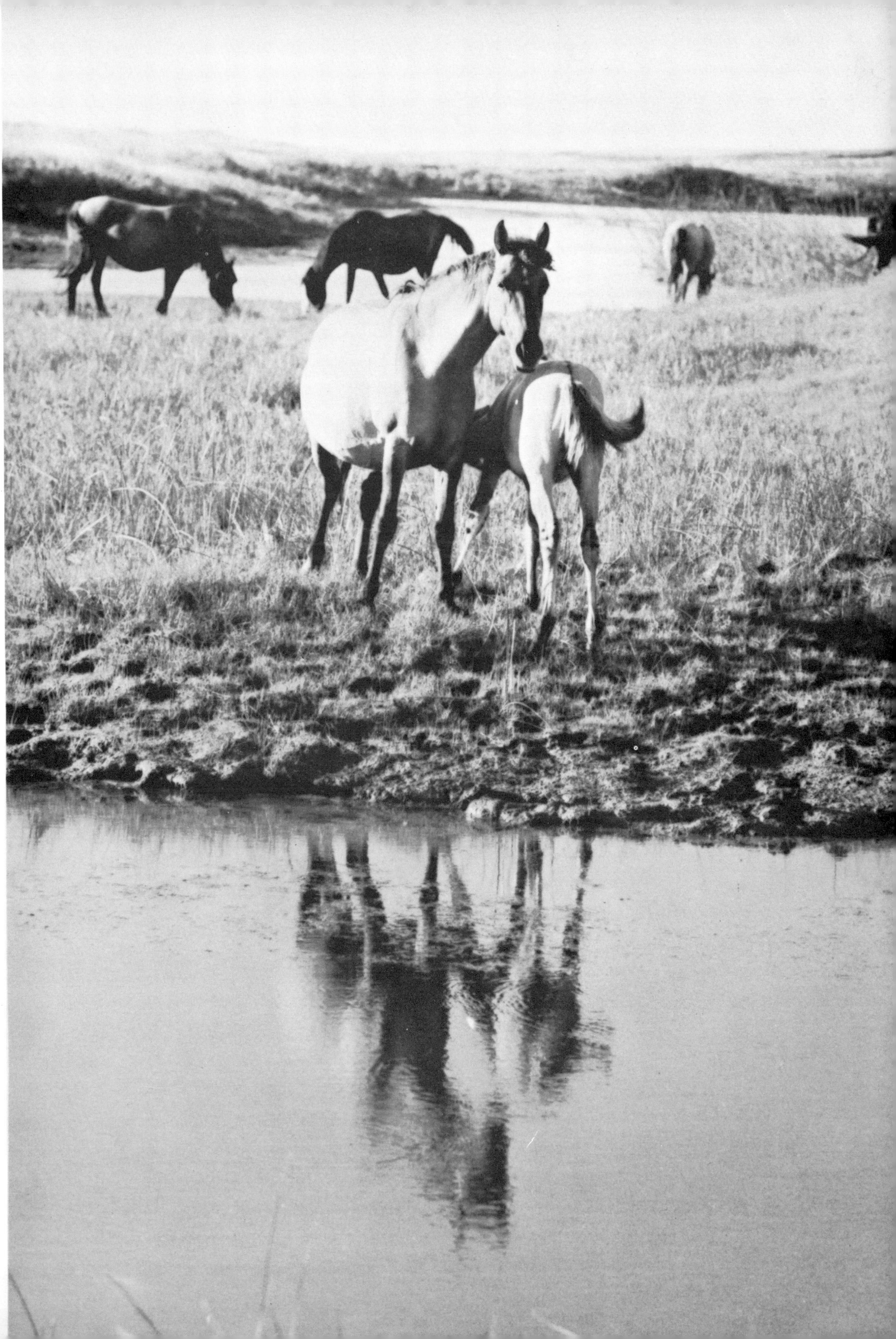

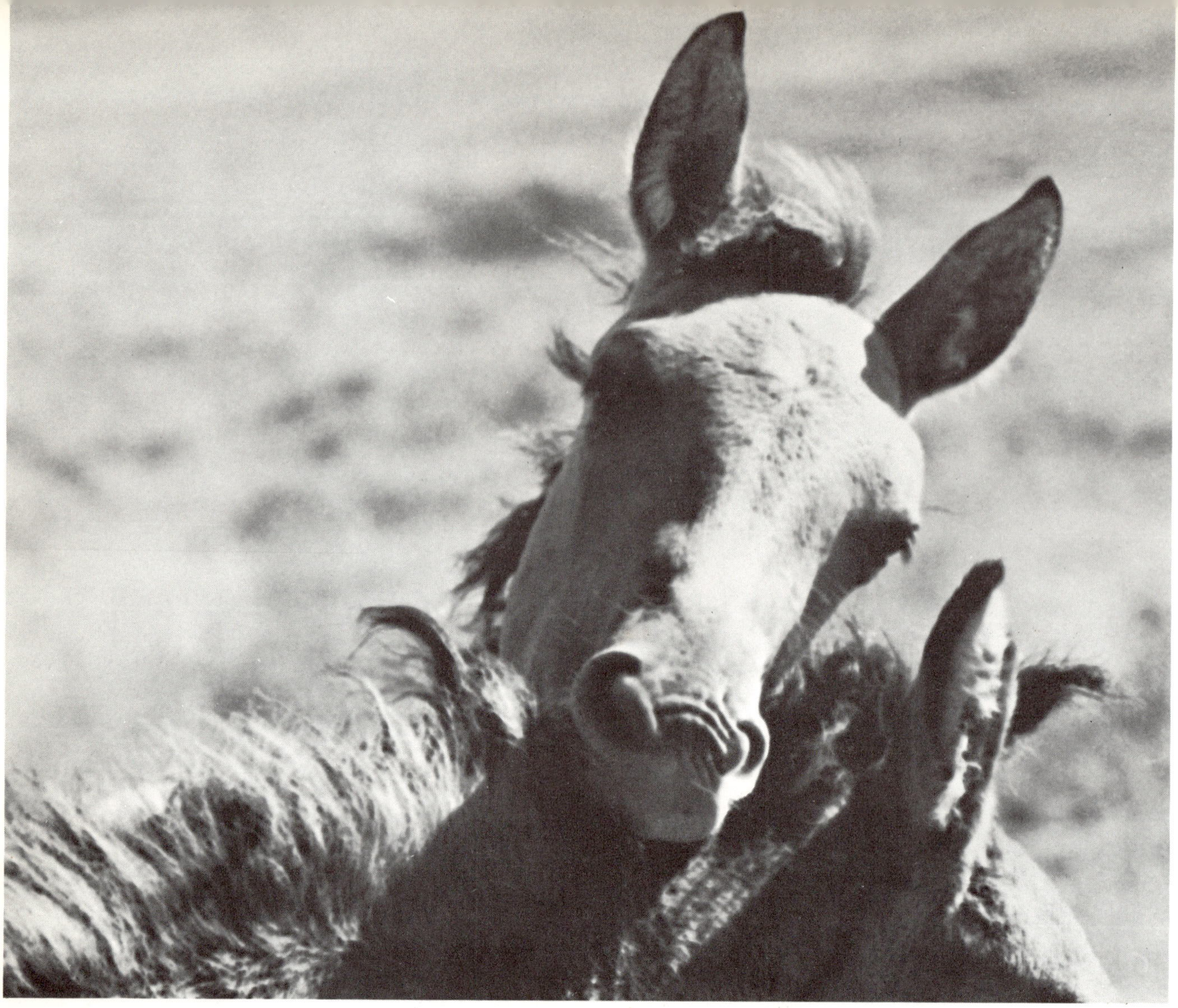

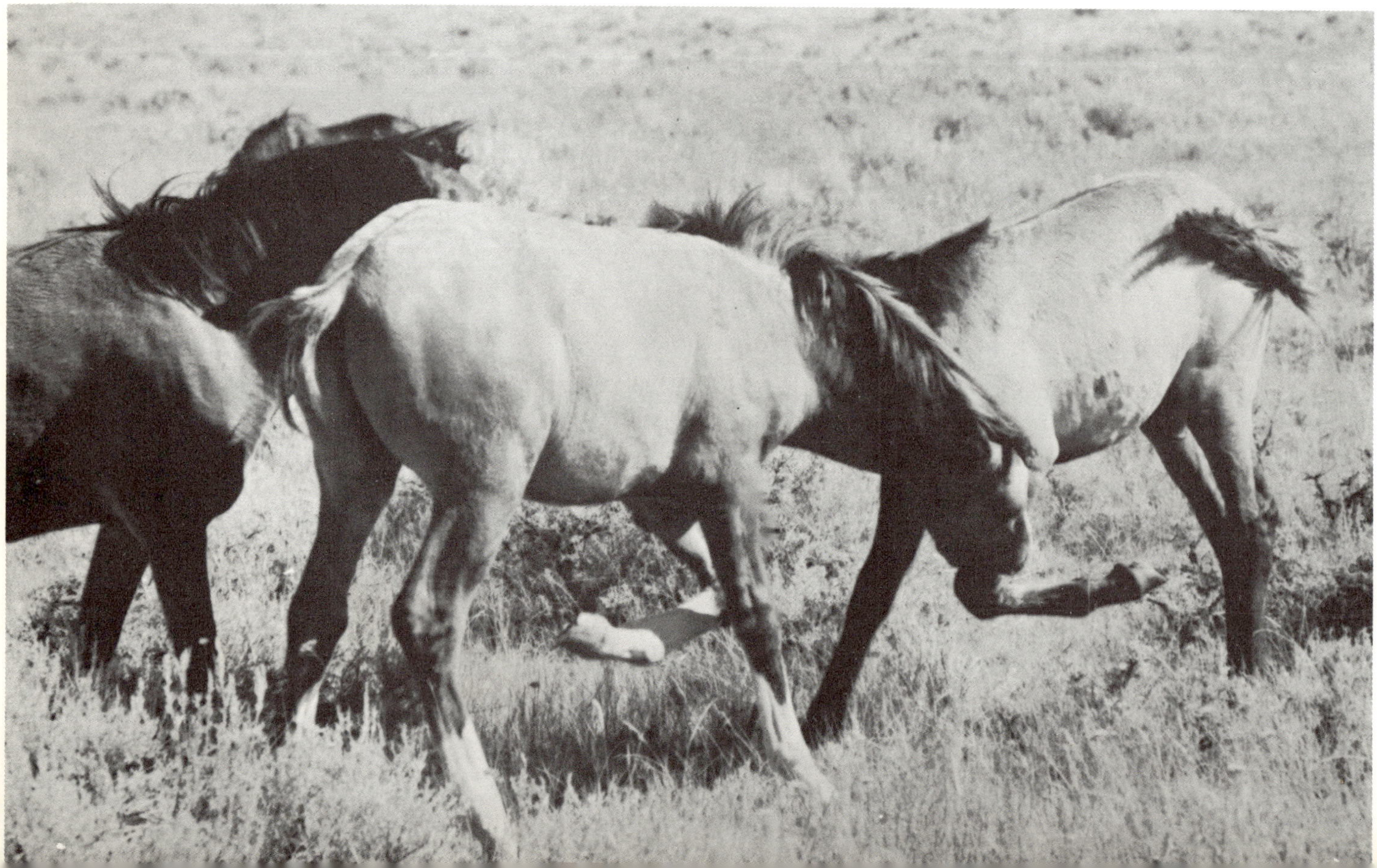

With so much protection, the wild colt could safely spend long hours at play with his brothers and sisters.

This time was valuable to the growing colts. It helped them to become strong. It also taught them how to fight . . . a lesson they needed to learn.

For the wild colt would soon have to fight in earnest. He was growing fast. Before long he would be a wild stallion himself. Then he would gather a harem of mares and have colts of his own to protect and teach and rescue from danger. His days of play would soon pass.

The wild colt was growing very fast.

The Author

HOPE RYDEN's love and understanding of animals and nature go back to her childhood. She grew up in western Illinois and spent every summer in northern Wisconsin, where the woods and wildlife occupied every waking moment.

Miss Ryden has been writing and producing feature films for TV since 1961 and was feature producer for ABC News from 1966 to 1968. Through John Walsh, special agent for the International Society for the Protection of Animals, she became involved in filming documentaries on such animal rescue projects as Operation Gwamba, which saved 10,000 wild animals from a flooded jungle in Surinam, South America, and a relief drop to 2,000 starving huskies in the Arctic Circle. And it was John Walsh who first told her about the herd of Pryor Mountain wild horses, which led to another documentary film and the writing of her award-winning book, *America's Last Wild Horses*, which was condensed in the *Reader's Digest*. Subsequently Miss Ryden helped draft a bill to protect the wild horses, testified before Senate and House committees. Her articles and photographs on the wild horses have appeared in the *National Geographic*, *Children's Day*, *National Park and Conservation Magazine*, *Time* magazine, and the New York *Times*.

Miss Ryden is presently at work on two books centering on the wild horse: an adult title featuring magnificent color photographs and a novel for young readers. Through her writing, photographs, and films, she wants to concentrate on making Americans aware of the plight of wild animals in danger of extinction in North America.